A Love That Surpasses
Living Loved-Fearless and Free

Sarah Lowry

Copyright © 2021 Sarah Lowry

All rights reserved.

ISBN: 9798459771220

DEDICATION

To my greatest joys, Hayden and Emmett.
You unveiled heaven on earth for me.

CONTENTS

	Acknowledgments	i
CHAPTER 1	Expecting Perfection	Pg. 1
CHAPTER 2	Finding Your Value in Surrender	Pg. 8
CHAPTER 3	All Chains Are Breakable	Pg. 15
CHAPTER 4	Choosing Grace Over Bitterness	Pg. 21
CHAPTER 5	Courage Through Faith	Pg. 26
CHAPTER 6	The Perseverance of Truth	Pg. 33
CHAPTER 7	Trading Jealousy for Joy	Pg. 38
CHAPTER 8	God on Display	Pg. 43
CHAPTER 9	A Love That Surpasses	Pg. 48
CHPATER 10	Living Loved	Pg. 53
	About the Author	Pg. 61

ACKNOWLEDGMENTS

I would like to open with thanking our Almighty God who has opened my eyes to see His glory and redeemed me from the dark places. I am thankful for Him flaming the fire in my heart to set His people free with His truth. I pray that many people, across the world, are blessed from the words inside this book and the hope I have put into sharing my story.

    I would like to express my deepest gratitude to my mother and her endless prayers over me during childhood-- that I would experience the fullness of God's love. My husband Dallas, who is always bringing out my courageous side and pushing me outside of my comfort zone. I would like to thank Megan Bouchillon, who was intricately placed into my life as a source of encouragement and edited this manuscript with love.

    Lastly to my children, Hayden and Emmett. Thank you for growing and stretching me in ways that have given me the deepest sense of purpose. The two of you have given me an abundance of joy and my love for you surpasses words. Through you both, nations will receive freedom in God's truth. God's glory will shine like the sun bright throughout desolate islands. I dedicate this book and verse below to you both. I love you.

"Before I formed you in the womb I knew you, before you were born, I set you apart; I appointed you as a prophet to the nations."

Jeremiah 1:5

INTRODUCTION

Devastation crashes down on us like a storm in the ocean and waves smother us when our future as we know it, changes permanently. I entered into a storm like this through a phone call, which I received on an ordinary Wednesday afternoon. This news would forever change my life and perspective. The doctor spoke softly on the other end of the phone, explaining that my noninvasive prenatal test (NIPT) results were in and that I was pregnant with a boy. A baby boy who has a positive screening for Down Syndrome.

Even with being a Christian and having faith in God, that didn't stop Satan from attacking me with deep fears and negative thoughts. Just as God's servant, Job, was oppressed, I felt as if Satan pounced at the opportunity to bound me in hopelessness. I found myself in my living room surrounded by darkness with a pillow soaked with tears. I remember thinking, "God, I know through faith that You are here but I can't sense Your presence through this suffocating, life-altering moment." Before I could stop myself, I prayed to God to allow me to miscarry if my son did in fact have Down syndrome. Just as I prayed this, I was filled with instant remorse. But God's grace showed me that His plans were bigger than my own and He was bigger than my thoughts- which were consumed with fear and were not actually true to my heart. That night, God brought me a dream that made the reality of that prayer to miscarry all too real. I found myself absolutely devastated over the loss of my son. I am so grateful for this dream because in it, I found relief. The pain of losing my son was far greater than the uncertainty of his diagnosis. I awoke knowing that my baby boy was not a mistake and that my son was given to me with intention and purpose. He was a gift.

    The rest of my pregnancy was a rollercoaster of ups and downs, faith and fear, until the day of my son's arrival- which God turned into a beautiful story full of love and redemption. We named our son Emmett and to our surprise, learned afterwards that his name means "truth" in Hebrew. Through our journey with Emmett, God's truth is exactly what has been revealed to us and it is the foundation on which we have planted our life in, and we have watched it flourish and grow in unexpected ways. Because of this experience and my continuous walk-through motherhood, I found myself asking "why" and bringing my worldly views of perfection into question. Why are we so dependent on such a broken idea of worth? How can we find God's grace through such suffocating fear of inadequacy and shame? How do we embrace His love in the midst of our immense guilt? Thankfully God is relentless, and He showed me that I was already free from the bondage of iniquity.

In this book, I invite you to walk alongside me as I uncover the lies that Satan tries to put into our hearts, the same lies he tried to use with me. Through biblical truth and my own experiences shared with you in this book; my hope is that you will realize your inheritance of freedom and how to live loved in a love that surpasses our understanding.

"In him and through faith in him we may approach God with freedom and confidence. ask you, therefore, not to be discouraged because of my sufferings for you, which are your glory.
For this reason, I kneel before the Father, from whom every family in heaven and on earth derives its name. I pray that out of his

glorious riches he may strengthen you with power through his Spirit in your inner being, so that Christ may dwell in your hearts through faith. And I pray that you, being rooted and established in love, may have power, together with all the Lord's holy people, to grasp how wide and long and high and deep is the love of Christ, and to know this love that surpasses knowledge—that you may be filled to the measure of all the fullness of God.

Now to him who is able to do immeasurably more than all we ask or imagine, according to his power that is at work within us, to him be glory in the church and in Christ Jesus throughout all generations, for ever and ever! Amen." Ephesians 3: 12-20

CHAPTER ONE:
EXPECTING PERFECTION

*"So God created mankind in his own image,
in the image of God he created them." Genesis 1:27*

Expectations are a funny thing. Some, we are consciously aware of, while others hide deep in our hearts. Oftentimes, we do not even know they are there until we are met with the realization that things won't become what you had hoped. I expected a child with 46 chromosomes. Having a child with 47 was not in my plan. My heart was a beautiful garden, full of plants blooming on the surface and unaware of what had been growing underneath. Obtaining a prenatal diagnosis of Down syndrome for our son was like God coming through that garden and pulling out all the weeds hiding under those beautiful plants. Leaving me to adjust my eyes to a new kind of beauty. Taking away my plans in preparation for His own. As the dust settled, I found my heart questioning why I had never seen the weeds under those flowers in the first place.

Why do we as parents expect perfection from our children? The excitement of finding out you are expecting a child is pure bliss. It leaves you to wonder who this child will grow up to be, who they will marry, and what accomplishments they will make on this earth. Maybe you dream they will follow in your footsteps with their career choices or take over the family business. We put so many expectations on our children from the beginning. Some of this idealization was even subconscious. When I found out Emmett would have Down syndrome; one of my first thoughts was he might not get married or have children. I subconsciously expected that of him. Many of us find out somewhere along our journey of parenthood that these grandiose ideas we have, while peering into our newborn's eyes, aren't always going to play out the way we believed that they would. Children grow up to make their own decisions and create their own paths that might not match up to what we originally had in mind for them. Then there are people like me: the select few of us that face this realization, our biggest fears, well before even meeting our precious child. I had such a moment, one that felt so unnatural, as I sat across the table from a doctor who made assumptions about my child's future and health. As you can imagine, this conversation crushes your very soul. Even at the mere thought of having a baby, we as parents subconsciously project the expectation of perfection over their lives.

For those of us that end up in this particular chair of unexpectedness, what place are we left in? I found myself in an isolated and desolate place. One filled with thoughts that left me in a state of anger, bitterness, jealousy, and fear of rejection. My view of the world and how it should be was taken and suddenly I was stripped of what I thought my perfect life should look like.

From where does the origins of our expectations of perfection come from though? I wasn't raised under such standards, but only to do my best. I had figured out by this point in my life that things were never as you expected them to be. Life never tends to be picture perfect. So why did I think I deserved a path of life that was much different than the one I was getting? We all seem to have this idea of excellence ingrained in us. There is almost this innate approach to everything in our lives that we must get it exactly right, our stuff should look like "this", and our achievements should measure up to "that."

God continued to pull out more weeds. I can imagine Him at this point saying, "Sarah, this weed has been overgrowing for far too long now. It's time to cut it all back. I'm pulling up this for my glory. Do you see My love yet? Oh wait, there's another big weed. Yep, that's got to go too!" As my eyes were opened by the pulling of weeds in my heart, for the first time I saw a parallel plane to our view of the world. The broken side of it that is intricately infused with sin and the one God originally wanted it to be one that is shared with Him. One that is perfect. In Genesis 1:27, when God created mankind, He created both man and woman in His image. The very mere of our existence was made out of His image, the epitome of perfection. God's character and very being is an all-encompassing perfection which he imputed into each of us. After the fall of mankind in the garden of Eden, sin caused separation from God and our pureness in Him was permanently marred. It's as if we long for the pureness of perfection out of which we were created. Even as parents we see glimpses of this pureness again in our babies. Holding them in our arms, we experience echoes of heaven on earth. Jesus speaks to this in Matthew 19:14, "the kingdom of heaven belongs to such as these." Our children are the innocence of God and thus the desires of hearts are to hold onto this for as long as we can, projecting beliefs formed out of sin onto ourselves and our children.

A LOVE THAT SURPASSES

Most parents get to subtly adjust their eyes to the paths their children have chosen as they grow; then there are the few whose dreams for their children get drastically taken away even before their little one takes their first breath. It can be gut wrenching and extremely wounding. My plans were so quickly snatched away, within minutes during a single phone call. It was a Wednesday afternoon when I had decided to lay down during my daughter's naptime. As I was drifting to sleep, I felt the vibrations of my cell phone ringing. I vaguely contemplated ignoring the phone call but decided to look and see who was calling before sending it to voicemail. I gasped for joy as I saw that it was my O.B. office because I knew our gender results were in. I had been waiting three weeks to find out the results. It didn't strike me as unusual that it was the doctor calling to relay my results. Again, there were zero expectations of our child having anything but a typical 46 chromosome screening result. Eagerly I answered the phone and said, "hello!" I was met by the doctor's soft voice, "Hi, Is this Sarah?" I responded, "Yes! This is she! Are our NIPT results in?" She only had time to say, "Yes, I am calling for your results." until I blurted in, "Oh, well don't tell me the gender. I would like to do a gender reveal party. Are you able to email me with the results?" She replied, "Yes, of course we can mail you this copy. I am so sorry, but I am calling to tell you that your screening came back positive for Trisomy 21 or otherwise known as Down syndrome." There was a long pause after her statement when I finally fumbled out the words, "yes, I know what Trisomy 21 is."

She began explaining the next steps such as referring me to the high-risk obstetric doctor for further imaging such as an ultrasound that would look for soft markers. The only thing I could think to ask her in my moment of shock was, "how accurate is this screening?" In her soft solum voice she said, "well, you are correct. It is only a screening, but these tests are 99% accurate for a Trisomy 21 diagnosis. It would be highly unlikely that in all actuality that this is a false positive result. You will be given the option to do an amniocentesis if you wish to find out an absolute diagnostic answer." My mind was spinning at this point and in desperation to know as much as possible about this child we would be having I asked her, "Okay, well I would like to know the gender now." In her attempt to make my pregnancy as normal as possible she kindly said, "it's okay, we can send you those results if you would still like to do your gender announcement." "No," I said, "please just go ahead and tell me." My heart was already so broken. I knew there would be no party or surprise gender announcement by cutting into a cake. All I wanted was to desperately look into our future to see what that would look like now. "Boy," She said, "You are going to have a boy."

A LOVE THAT SURPASSES

While my unexpected pivot in life comes from a prenatal diagnosis of Down syndrome, there are so many different ways that this happens to other families. A child may receive a diagnosis of autism, cancer, or chronic illness or perhaps later in life, a child takes his own life, joins a gang or becomes an addict. And just as devastatingly, some families never meet their little one, whether they miscarry or are unable to carry due to infertility or other factors. My unexpected change in plans might look different than my neighbors, but we all have something in common. We share a common feeling that life wasn't supposed to be this way. Many of us are left wondering why or may find themselves resenting God. Some of us feel so much shame and guilt that we begin to believe that they were always undeserving, unworthy of a happy life all along.

For those who do not know me or are reading my story for the first time, I am a Pediatric Oncology nurse and certified Pediatric Nurse Practitioner. One Friday while at work, it was just me and this other nurse in the lab. We accessed children's central lines and then would send them on their way for chemotherapy infusions or to see their doctor. As mothers do, the nurse and I began to talk about our children and I shared our story about my son Emmett, who was 18 months at the time. We found ourselves talking about faith and my calling to start a nonprofit in hopes of helping other families who are going through what I experienced. I tried my best to explain to her how I viewed my son and his disability, but I was unable to find the right words. I wanted to explain just how deep and complex all of the feelings were but until now, I couldn't figure out how to help her to understand. But now, as I write this, the words I so desperately couldn't find come so clearly as I relate with each of you. I think most parents who have a child with a disability would agree that they, too, experience so much joy and love in a deep but complex way.

As all of our children are made up of our own hearts that live outside our body; we recognize the fear of anything happening to our hearts. We want to protect them and shelter them from such a cruel world. Having a child with a disability, makes this world turn black in an instant. The lights are shut off and you are placed in foreign waters trying to protect your heart which is your child. What once was a place full of wonder turns into a place of rejection for your whole family. The love you have for your child gets confusing because it is such a great love, but this love is also deeply painful. If we were given a choice, we would try to avoid pain at all costs because the fear of pain can be smothering. However, it's not humanly possible to avoid it. Sin has now entered our world and with sin comes pain and suffering. We are constantly fed lies that burden us daily in our walk of this life. However, there is a secret and a key that allows us to view past this brokenness and to disarm these lies.

A LOVE THAT SURPASSES

It is our rightful inheritance in Christ.

This place that you have wandered down might be filled with desperation but when you open your eyes, you'll see the rich beauty in it. The best way that I can explain it is this: Imagine you are making a delicious vegetable soup. You get the carrots, celery, beans, potatoes, and maybe some onions. Each ingredient being full of flavor and bringing an array of color to the dish. How about the onion? Meaning, how would you describe the onion? Most appear rather dull, flakey even. Not really exciting in comparison to the other ingredients. Not to mention, onions typically make you cry as you pull back the layers. Maybe you already know where I am going with this.

It would have been easier to leave out the onion. There would have been less crying, perhaps. Maybe you would have decided to leave the onion out based solely on its appearance. Its peeling outer layer and strong fumes might appear an unlikely addition to your tasty soup. But we both know what we would be missing without the rich flavor the onions bring to the dish and not to mention the immense health benefits it adds to any dish.

If I were writing my own story, I would have been tempted to not add the onion in my life, or in this case, a diagnosis. But thankfully God is the author, and He added an ingredient to my life that was of infinite value. Emmett's diagnosis was not so appealing on the outside. But as I've peeled back the layers of all this, I have found truth, God's truth. And He has revealed where I placed my beliefs and how I adopted so much of the world's definition of worth.

We went back and forth on what to name Emmett while pregnant. The only name my husband and I seemed to agree on was Emmett but even then, we were still so unsure. When Emmett was about six months old, we moved across the country, and I started a new job. I was introduced to a new coworker who happened to be Jewish. We started talking about our children, I told her Hayden and Emmett's names and their ages. She immediately interrupted and told me, "Oh, Emmett means "truth" in Hebrew!" So the person who has taught me more about God's unconditional love, his name literally means truth. God knew my heart needed some peace about where He was leading me and this was definitely one of those moments for me.

If I were writing my own story, I would have been tempted to not add the onion in my life, or in this case, a diagnosis.

But thankfully God is the author, and He added an ingredient to my life that was of infinite value.

Emmett's diagnosis was not so appealing on the outside.

I think most of us can agree that there is just something so special about individuals with Down syndrome and their ability to retain an innocent perspective throughout their lives. After some in depth thinking, the only word I could come up with to truly describe this difference was the word, "pure." But why? Suddenly the reason why dawned on me, it's because there is no deception in their love. Individuals with Down syndrome don't love you for any type of status gain but instead love you whether you're a nobody or a somebody. This love from a pure heart is the closest thing we have to Jesus' love on this earth. Matthew 5:8 says, "Blessed are the pure in heart, for they will see God." Through my son's ability to display a unique innocence, he reveals a layer of God's pureness in love that I might have otherwise missed in this world. I thought my eyes were open, but I was truly blind before having Emmett.

As we close this first chapter, I hope I can bring that same peace and reassurance for you. I pray that this book can be a continuation of Emmett's purpose in my life; to point to the truth and to open your eyes to God's love and His sweet freedom.

"When hard pressed, I cried to the LORD; he brought me into a spacious place." - *Psalm 118:5*

LIVING LOVED PRAYER:

"Lord, thank you for your unexpected blessings. Mold my heart to be filled with the love only you can provide and open my eyes to your ways. Help me to stand firm in your truth and focus on praiseworthy thoughts. Amen."

CHAPTER TWO:
FINDING YOUR VALUE IN SURRENDER

"Then Jesus said to his disciples, "Whoever wants to be my disciple must deny themselves and take up their cross and follow me. For whoever wants to save their life will lose it, but whoever loses their life for me will find it." Matthew 16:24-25

I would describe myself as ignorant, blind, before I had Emmett. Not my fault or yours. Until you've received an experience that changes your perspective entirely, by flipping your world as you know it upside down, you just can't put yourself in those shoes. My dear sweet boy, Emmett, he makes this world so much clearer. We don't even realize how we unintentionally consider the value of others through worldly ideals and measures of success. Google defines the word value as, "One's judgement of what is important in life; the regard that something is held to deserve, the importance, worth, or usefulness of something." When God gave Emmett to me, He didn't just give me a son, he gave me a glimpse of just how broken our world is and how blinded we all truly are even as Christians.

When I was pregnant, I heard so many people, who meant well, tell me, "But babies who have Down syndrome are the cutest." I would nod my head in agreement but in the back of my mind I wondered: *Will you think my son is cute when he's an adult? Are you seeing his true worth because looks will fade? Will you see his value if one day he is helping you bag your groceries at the store? Will you know how proud I am of him for doing that job because someone saw past his disability and saw the value of what he has to offer?* These questions and thoughts alone cause a deep pain out of fear of rejection for him. I don't lose many tears over him being a baby. That's the *easy* part. When I see any person who has a disability working in a job, I immediately think of how proud their mother is of them. How hard they've worked to get this job that so many other people would deem the value of their contribution to this world as insignificant. Applying for jobs in the past used to be so simple to me. You likely fill out an application online, filling in the blanks and *click click* it's done! Now I dread seeing the end of that form. You know the part at the end where it asks if you have a disability? I get to this part and feel nauseous. Like someone punched me in the gut because I know my son will always have to check that box. Most job applications provide a disclaimer promising that the company does not discriminate against disabilities, but they do. They *just* did. They make you disclose that personal information before even agreeing to meet you in person. My heart swells with the feelings of rejection, just with one single page on a form or rather one box asking for a simple yes or no answer. To me, this question severely undervalues someone who has a disability and what they have to bring to the table, well before they are even given a chance.

We moved to the heart of Silicon Valley in October of 2019. The movers had arrived at our new home to unpack our belongings and I needed to go to the employee health department of my new job at Stanford, to finish my new hire paperwork. My husband and I agreed to divide up the kids and so I took Emmett with me while our daughter Hayden stayed back home with him. My car was still being shipped from Nashville, so I was forced to take an Uber to our destination. On the way home from our appointment, our Uber driver was a kind man in his 50s who easily engaged with us in conversation. I explained how we had just moved here and only stepped off the plane a mere three days ago from Nashville, Tennessee. His face lit up and he said, "Oh wow, I am a southerner too. I'm actually from Florida." The topic of the conversation was then shifted towards the difference between Silicon Valley and the South. "How do you like it here so far?" he asked. "Well, I only stepped off the plane two days ago. I'm too new to the area to gage the differences. In fact, I just feel like I am on vacation at this point." He chuckled and said, "well you will notice there is a big cultural difference between the two areas." "Oh really? How so?" I asked. He went on to explain the number one difference he noticed was that everyone wants to flaunt their success here. He said, "You will notice they drive nice cars, have nice houses, talk a lot about themselves, and their career accomplishments." I nodded while listening to him continue to speak but there were no words I had left to say. All I could think was how I couldn't believe we had just moved to what seems to be one of the vainest places to live in the country with our two children who had delays. Suddenly, the fight to defend my children's value seemed like a mountain to climb.

That mountain formed into one as tall as Mount Everest one day while I was sitting at work. One of my sweet coworkers, a nurse and mother of three, was expressing how frustrating it is to be a parent here in this community. She went on to describe how her son's teacher was pushing for him to be better in math. She explained her son is an average student but here in the Bay Area, that is just not good enough. Average is viewed poorly, and parents are pushing their children to be nothing short of exceptional. She explained how parents put their children in a ton of after school activities such as piano, sports, and gymnastics. All to increase their chances of getting into an Ivy league school such as Stanford. It made her so sad to see the amount of pressure her "typical" child faced at school because of this culture of great excellence. She continued to share a story regarding another mom she knew, whose daughter's first grade class had a "career" day at school. All of the kids were saying what they wanted to be when they grew up. This mother had overheard another little boy in the class tell his mom that he wanted to become a pilot. In turn, his mother's response to him was, "you will *not* be a pilot. Pilots are glorified Uber drivers." Is your mouth open in gaping disbelief right now? Mine sure was when I heard this story for the first time too.

As I think back on how these stories and situations made me feel, how in those moments I was left with a sinking heart. I found myself thinking how my children weren't going to be accepted or valued. That if they didn't meet certain standards, other people in this area we now live in were going to deem them worthless and not good enough. Especially if children who don't have any delays are struggling to succeed in these high demand school atmospheres. These are the perfect moments to know when to take a step back and ask yourself, "who is this storyline coming from?" Most importantly, is this what God's truth says about myself or my child? The answer is no. These are lies being intricately placed into your mind by Satan. Lies that are fueling self-righteousness and pride. Who does God deem worthy? Only the highest achievers? Only the best? Jesus mostly chose people who were deemed unworthy and didn't have the success of money to become His greatest leaders for His kingdom. The measure of success in this world and the heavenly realm has two completely different definitions. When we surrender our lives to him daily and humble ourselves by serving others; we find an abundance more that fills us with worth and happiness through sharing the glory of God with others. We find true wholeness and oneness with God who deems us incredibly valued. Dear friend, your value will never fade because you are not defined by the world's definition of it. Your very existence has been created by an Almighty God and you were made in His image. His good and perfect image, to which only He determines

Then come follow me.

your worth. We are continuously in a war for our minds but if we hold on to God's truths tight, we can dismantle the lies that we come face against.

How do we choose to live in God's truth, remain in humility, and surrender the control we hold over our lives? We could start by reframing our questions. What if we didn't ask our children what they wanted to be when they grow up? Instead asking them, "Whose life do you want to make an impact on and how are you going to reach that goal?" What if we fostered the culture of kindness in our children? Ensuring that they are able to see when another child is being bullied, left out, and excluded from the group. Teaching our children that there is more to life than trying to be the best, only out of your own self-interest, versus striving to be your best self with the motive to impact others in a positive way. What parents pour God's love into their children for the betterment of the human race? Encouraging them that even those who were created differently from them were perfect in the eyes of our creator. The glory of God would burn bright in our children through their humility, acceptance, and servant hearts.

Somewhere along the way we have misconstrued blessings as personal gains through our own means instead of viewing them as gifts that He grants us for our time here on earth. In Matthew 19:21, Jesus tells us to sell our possessions and give to others; that by doing this we will have treasure in heaven. It is after these instructions that He tells us to, "Then come, follow me," indicating we must give up these parts of ourselves before we can faithfully follow in His footsteps. But Sarah, isn't this statement in the bible only for the rich; the ones whose hearts are filled with greed? Glad you asked! Jesus actually said this to all of us. What is He truly telling us though? He's telling us to surrender to Him by denying our self-righteousness, self-interest, and idols. By surrendering our children, health, marriage, materialistic items, and our dreams; we become faithful in trusting only in Him to provide for us. By relinquishing control over these things that become idols in our lives and surrendering it all for God's glory; we can expect our blessings to increase tenfold. He will part the waters for your big dream. He will shut the mouth of the lions in your path. He will provide the faith to keep moving forward through the desolate places you have to walk. An abundance of success through Jesus is waiting for you but it can only be achieved only through surrendering and opening our eyes to value as defined by our wonderful creator. Through this process, you will find healing and the strength to move the mountains in which you find yourself facing. We *truly succeed* in this life by setting our minds towards impacting others for *His* glory and not our own.

So next time we are faced with questioning our value, let us remember who is feeding us those lies. We don't have to stay in that place where we feel cast aside. Our Lord has spoken. He sings His love and worth over your life. It's time to stand back up and in your faith expose those lies by claiming your value through surrendering it to Jesus. Freedom from this comes only through surrendering to God's truth and His truth says you are loved, valued, and worthy. This truth is your rightful inheritance, and it can never be taken from you!

"There is no one who can rescue from My power. I act and who can reverse it." Isaiah 43:12-13

LIVING LOVED PRAYER:

"Father, help me to see the beauty and value of every individual in this world that you have created including my own. I rebuke the world's definition of value based on ability and self-gain. I choose to pick up my cross today to follow you. I release my old ways of defining worth by surrendering everything in my life including my health, marriage, children, and dreams. I am worthy because You say I am and who can reverse Your words? (Isaiah 43:12-13) Fill my heart with your grace and open my eyes to see the shining Glory of Your work that's being intricately woven into my life now. Amen."

A LOVE THAT SURPASSES

Dearest Friend,

You are loved by Christ. You are part of the greatest love story and His love for you is bigger than any crashing wave. His love, like a wave, breaks down all lies of unworthiness. Your worth and value as an individual is not even fathomable. When shame says, "I am a mistake," God says, "My love for you surpasses knowledge." As a parent of a child with a disability, we so desperately want other people to view our children through our own eyes. Our eyes which are filled with love and our hearts which swell with their worth anytime we imagine our precious child's face. We always see them first and never their disability. Don't you think this is the exact same way God feels about you?

We tend to see ourselves as unworthy; we allow ourselves to believe the standards which this broken world constitutes as worthy. However, the truth of the matter is that your worth and value are not associated with any action that you could take or what you can accomplish. Christ breathed His life into you and in that same breath entered His love. In His love, He sings over you, He crowns you in beauty, and He knows you by your name. Know this, embrace this, and live freely through this unconditional love.

Blessings,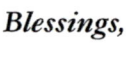

CHAPTER THREE:
ALL CHAINS ARE BREAKABLE

"Be strong, do not fear; your God will come, he will come with vengeance; with divine retribution he will come to save you." Then will the eyes of the blind be opened and the ears of the deaf unstopped." Isaiah 35:4-5

It was three years of a seemingly endless road of rejection, shame, and deep wounds where I had continually asked God, "Why are you allowing this to happen? What is your lesson through these multiple rejections?" My close loved ones would comfort me by saying this just wasn't the right opportunity for me and my perfect job was out there somewhere. I was extremely dissatisfied with this simple answer. Deep down I felt like there was a bigger reason for this heavy and shameful season.

During the summer of 2017, I had graduated with my master's in nursing and passed my certification boards to be a Pediatric Nurse Practitioner. My last year of school was filled by working the night shift as a Pediatric Oncology Nurse, doing my clinical rotation hours at the Pediatricians office, and finding out that I was pregnant with our first child. I gave birth to our beautiful daughter in April and after three weeks postpartum, during my maternity leave, I went back to finish my grad school clinicals in order to graduate. That saying "mama's tired" took a whole new level that year. There were so many tears and words of encouragement from my husband and parents that brought me to the finish line that was graduation. To say I was proud of finishing my masters through all of that is an understatement. I'll never forget the day that I stood on the porch telling my mother to take a picture of me while holding my four-month-old and the certificate that stated I had passed my boards. At this moment, I thought this was my career path and that this was everything that I was ever meant to be. This was my life's purpose, and I was sure of it! One by one, my other classmates obtained jobs and stepped into the promotion of their new roles. While there was never a lull in requests for various physician practices asking me to interview with them; the months after graduation turned into years and I was continually denied and rejected. The feedback I received varied from place to place. I heard that I lacked the experience that I needed to work in the specialty of pediatric oncology where I had focused my passions and put seven years of bedside experience into. Others would inform me that I had too much acute care experience for a primary care outpatient job.

The hardest rejection came after applying for a Nurse practitioner position in the outpatient area which I was currently working for a year and had gotten to know the team well. I had just gotten off work and we were in the backyard playing with the kids when the manager called me. She explained that they had hired someone else who used to work there and was coming back. In her best effort to let me down easily, she explained how I was already making the same pay that I would be making as a nurse practitioner so if I liked my job working as a floor nurse, I could always stay doing that. She said how it was very hard to obtain a position without experience and based the inability to hire me on this reason. I found out later that this manager had decided to hire a different new graduate who had zero bedside experience into another role which I had applied for within the same team and never was given a chance to interview for. It turns out that you can get a job in this career field easily without any bedside experience if your family is a big donor to the hospital.

I felt so much shame from not being able to obtain one of these positions especially when my classmates and coworkers knew I had this degree that I wanted to be practicing in but couldn't catch a break. I felt like God owed me an answer. It was after this huge disappointing event that I found myself asking Him, "Why am I being denied this? I thought this is the path that You wanted me to take. Please God, give my heart some peace and give me insight to the lesson You are teaching me."

It was a cool California morning, nice and sunny, as I drove into work. I was really struggling to go back into work and face the people who didn't want me on their team. I decided to call my mom on the way. We began talking about how Emmett had changed our perspectives on a lot of things in life. Then out of nowhere it hit me. I felt God speak into my life at that moment saying, "Sarah, I have been teaching you through Emmett, that

A LOVE THAT SURPASSES

It made so much sense and I could see so clearly now.

he is worthy, despite the rejection he will face, and so are you!" I suddenly had this unveiling of how much of my own worth that I had placed into obtaining this role. I felt as though I wasn't going to be successful or deemed worthy until I was practicing as a nurse practitioner, and I was unknowingly placing all of my value into this. It made so much sense and I could see so clearly now.

Through exposing this lie, I had been telling myself for so many years, I was finally able to move past the rejection and shame into the truth. The truth that we are worthy despite our failures. After coming to this realization, I started to think about how many other people were doing the same thing but through different circumstances. I have a girlfriend at work who I typically talk about Christianity with, and we share God's work in our lives. I began to ask her the same question, "What is something that you are letting define your life right now?" Her answer, as a single 30-year-old woman, was her relationship status. She went on to say she expected to be married with children by this point in her life. She felt like her mother was disappointed that she was in her thirties and didn't have any kind of serious relationship at all. She felt as though she was putting her life's value into obtaining this dream of being a wife and a mother. As we were speaking about this topic, she realized how much shame that she felt not having obtained this expected milestone in life yet. She also carried so much guilt that this undesired circumstance was her fault. We began to talk about dismantling these lies that take hold of us so tightly. There are so many different ways that the lie of shame and guilt can grab hold of our lives. Once we are able to unveil our eyes and see these lies are from the devil himself; only then will we see our true calling. We will then be able to see that our worth isn't measured by a job title or relationship status.

One of my favorite verses growing up was Psalms 139:14. "I praise you because I am fearfully and wonderfully made." I remember seeing all the girls in college having this tattooed on their body somewhere in a cursive font, either on their foot or side. It's a beautiful verse but what exactly does it mean to be "fearfully and wonderfully made?" The definition of fearfully in Hebrew defines it as: with great reverence and heart felt interest and respect. Then the word wonderfully in Hebrew is defined as: unique, set apart, and uniquely marvelous. We are so quick to proclaim this biblical truth but somewhere along the way the lies make it easy to forget the depth of it. When the devil chains you to shame and guilt, he prides himself on making his lies seem bigger than the depth of your uniquely marvelous and set apart life. Open your eyes to realize the God, who set you apart, has designed every single one of your days. You were made with great reverence, and we can be joyous in our weaknesses because through Jesus it has no hold on our lives!

The chains of fear are another tactic that Satan loves to use as a trap. My daughter Hayden has never been the fearful type. In fact, she would often not notice dangerous situations and we would have to be helicopter parents that watched her every move when we were out somewhere. She would wander deeper and deeper into the ocean, sprint out into the middle of the road, or even attempt to pet a strangers' large dog at the park. Hayden was the definition of fearless. She never questioned her safety.

Our parenting journey with Hayden hasn't always been easy. As a Certified Pediatric Nurse Practitioner, I noticed she wasn't meeting her communication milestones around nine months old when she should have been mimicking by pointing or waving. My concerns were dismissed multiple times by her pediatrician until around 15 months old when I self-referred her into our early intervention state program. We were immediately enrolled into speech therapy twice a week and told she had a global communication delay. She is always a very happy child but heavily in her own world. This was a very heavy season we walked through with her. We followed through with multiple appointments and testing which might tell us why these delays were happening but none of them could. We were given no answers from doctors except for the fact that she was probably just a late bloomer, meanwhile every therapist we saw to help her catch up, projected their unwarranted opinions of her to us. The unknown of why she was delayed instilled so much fear and anxiety regarding her future into our hearts and we walked through a very heavy season because of it. The fear was so heavy during this time that I feel like I was robbed of part of her childhood.

By the age of three and a half, we finally got settled from our move across the country and enrolled Hayden into school. School became the best therapy she'd ever received, and she loved every minute of it. Her vocabulary soared and with it so did her increase in engagement and awareness. We were finally seeing her come outside of her own bubble and into the world. We noticed she entered into a new phase where she was becoming curious and even fearful of things. A typical developmental milestone in childhood that we were glad to see her reach, but it was as if Hayden's eyes were opened, and she was awakened. This new phase reminded me so much of a particular part in Adam and Eve's story. After they had eaten the forbidden fruit, their awareness was awakened. In Genesis 3:7, it says their eyes were opened. Only then did they realize and experience the fear and shame which was sin. Once the door for sin was opened in their hearts it allowed Satan to fill their minds with this fear and shame. We are just like Adam and Eve in today's world when we allow sin into our lives as it fills our heart with lies. There are times where these lies are so intricate and beautifully formed, we don't even realize where they are actually coming from. When we aren't spiritually awake, we do not realize the power we obtain through Jesus, so we struggle to dispel these ideas and to recognize the grip it has on our lives. When God was walking through the Garden of Eden and found them scared and full of shame He said to them, "Who told you that?" I love this question because the Bible makes it clear that God did not speak these words into them. Growing up my mother would ask me this exact same question. I remember being so defeated and discouraged when I was rejected from things such as friends or jobs. As I was speaking these untruths, that I wasn't good enough to fit in or obtain that particular job; she would stop me and say, "But who told you that?"

Take a second to stop and analyze where your negative thoughts are coming from and find the real truth. Even though our eyes are opened, and we see the great fear in our world; we should rest in God's truth that this fear is not from Him, nor are we created with a spirit of fear. In this same truth, He has granted us access to His almighty power to unleash Satan's grip over us. Your eyes were opened to sin, but have they opened yet to the one who conquered that sin? Do you know what this means for you? It means all chains are breakable in Jesus' name. All chains!

LIVING LOVED PRAYER:

"Jesus, I acknowledge your power and sovereignty. I am done carrying these heavy chains of fear and shame. I declare in your name Jesus to be released from these chains today. Break them for me so that I can live freely in your love. Fill me with your spirit so that I may remember how worthy I am in your sight. Amen."

CHAPTER FOUR:
CHOOSING GRACE OVER BITTERNESS

"He who was seated on the throne said, "I am making everything new!" Then he said, "Write this down, for these words are trustworthy and true." Revelation 21:5

There is a picture that resurfaces on my social media memories page once a year. It haunts me when I look at it because even though I was a Christian and went to church, I was still very much spiritually asleep. When I look at this picture of my husband and I with our daughter, sharing the announcement of our second child, I can barely recognize that it's us in the photograph. My heart sinks at the emotional trauma that had not yet occurred. This picture depicts our lives before the heartache that broke us and then the journey of healing from God by which He sewed us back together again. The journey that would reveal His almighty truth and grace in our lives.

When the plans for our children are so drastically different than what we had anticipated, it's hard not to blame yourself or ask why. This was a conversation a coworker had with me regarding her adult daughter who has autism. She told me that it's difficult to fathom how some couples who have multiple children only have to worry about life's typical struggles. She didn't sugarcoat it when she told me that she felt cheated in a way. If I have learned anything from this journey it's that those feelings of cheat quickly mold from the emotion of anger into bitterness towards others, because I too have fallen victim to that mindset. I remember scrolling through my social media accounts to see mothers posting photographs of their children meeting milestones so quickly. Anger seemed to seep out of my skin at the thought that they had never been on the other side talking to a high-risk doctor, never known the challenges of balancing therapy appointments, making individualized education plans, or strategizing daily play into therapy. They have never had to defend their child's value to society by constantly reminding others to view their children as a person first and their diagnosis second. It's almost mind baffling at the idea of such an easy life. The feelings of anger always precede bitterness. You see, anger happens initially and resides quicker. But bitterness, this emotion sinks it's claws deep into our hearts. This feeling stays months and sometimes even years if we let it. One thing I have realized on my unique journey parenting a child with a disability is that this doesn't only apply to mothers who have children with special needs.

As a pediatric nurse and certified nurse practitioner, I have worked with children for almost a decade and specifically in the oncology specialty. This career gives me a unique front row seat to some of the parents who I was envying. They birthed typical children and after a few years of loving them, their lives were turned upside down. Taking care of a family who has just received a diagnosis that their child has cancer is one of the most emotionally draining assignments a nurse can have. It is one of the biggest honors as well, to be able to sit with them in these intense moments that they will remember for the rest of their lives. As you can imagine, this profession has given me an incredible perspective and has been an incredibly humbling experience. We are never guaranteed the life we think we deserve and never promised a tomorrow. It was this perspective that broadened my horizons to realize that these parents of medically ill children, who have "typical" children, feel the exact same way.

I began thinking that if parents of children who have cancer feel this way, then how many other situations do people feel the anger within themselves that they have been cheated and leaving them with long term bitterness? I started realizing the mother whose child was raised in love and died in a tragic accident, became addicted to drugs, committed suicide, ran away from home, committed a crime, or joined a violent gang, probably all felt immense bitterness. I can only imagine in these situations as well, that families grieved these losses and felt incredibly cheated of their expectation of their future too. The future that they wanted which was permanently ripped away from them in an instant. One of my favorite quotes that particularly resonates with my heart on this topic is written by C.S. Lewis and his description of the quaint home we are expecting to live in. It is comfortable, cozy, and we are pretty content with our small cottage. Then God comes in and fixes minor things along the way and we usually can easily adjust. But when He starts knocking down the walls, making big renovations, it gets quite uncomfortable. Maybe you're even questioning and angry with

We are never guaranteed the life we think we deserve and never promised a tomorrow.

his choices. The mess from all of the dirt can be extremely overwhelming too. The dust from the demolition can be lingering as well. Making this job a long-term project--most likely not on your timeline. Then we are left with a choice. Choose to stay in the unknown or in this case, the reminisce of unwanted dust and dirt. Remain in the mess and refuse to move forward—ultimately leaving you bitter or, you can choose to accept God's grace. The latter provides a new strength and patience to allow God to work and to witness when the dust finally settles, revealing His great handiwork, a palace. A palace created just for you and one that He will reside in to be closer to you.

"Imagine yourself as a living house. God comes in to rebuild that house. At first, perhaps, you can understand what He is doing. He is getting the drains right and stopping the leaks in the roof and so on; you knew that those jobs needed doing and so you are not surprised. But presently He starts knocking the house about in a way that hurts abominably and does not seem to make any sense. What on earth is He up to? The explanation is that He is building quite a different house from the one you thought of - throwing out a new wing here, putting on an extra floor there, running up towers, making courtyards. You thought you were being made into a decent little cottage: but He is building a palace. He intends to come and live in it Himself." - C.S Lewis

How do we find God's grace through our undesired home remodel? In 1 Peter 5, we are told that the God of all grace, who has called us to His eternal glory, will allow us to endure suffering. Once we have suffered a little while or enduring the mess of making a house a home; He restores Himself in us. He builds us up to be stronger, firm, and steadfast. The passage goes on to explain that believers all over the world will undergo similar suffering but through faith we obtain His grace to sustain us. Faith in Jesus is our secret key! Jesus sees you on the boat in the storm like the disciples in Mark 4:35. He sees you scared amidst the waves, but He is throwing a lifebuoy to you. In this story from the bible, Jesus is on the boat asleep during a storm. His disciples were terrified and also angry with him. How could he possibly be sleeping at a time like this? They woke Him up due to their terror. Jesus immediately rebuked the wind and waves upon awakening.

He made all things calm again. Then He looked at his disciples and said, "Why are you so afraid? Do you still have no faith?" He says it so plainly. And just as simplified, it is through our faith in Jesus, that we are able to turn our suffering into joy, fears into courage, anger and bitterness into grace, and worries into peace. He tells us in Luke 17 that we only need faith the size of a mustard seed and He will grow it for us. If you have faith in Him, you can offer up the anger and bitterness to calm the storm inside your heart too.

LIVING LOVED PRAYER:

"Jesus, I give you any doubts in my faith today. You see me on the boat in this storm filled with anger, fear, and confusion. I give you my anger and bitterness that has been brewing like a storm inside of my heart. I rebuke anger and bitterness in the name of Jesus. Be gone from my heart today. There is no place for these feelings here anymore. Lord, fill these empty places with your grace; grace for myself and grace for others in my life. Thank you for loving me and setting me free today. And so it shall be, in your name Jesus, Amen."

CHAPTER FIVE:
COURAGE THROUGH FAITH

"You intended to harm me, but God intended it for good to accomplish what is now being done, the saving of many lives." Genesis 50:20

Devastation crashes down on us like a storm in the ocean and waves smother us when our future as we know it changes permanently. I entered into a storm like this through a phone call, which I received on an ordinary Wednesday afternoon. This news would forever change my life and perspective. The doctor spoke softly on the other end of the phone explaining that my noninvasive prenatal test (NIPT) results were in and that I was pregnant with a boy. A baby boy who has a positive screening for Down Syndrome.

Even with being a Christian and having faith in God, that didn't stop Satan from attacking me with deep fears and negative thoughts. Just as God's servant Job was oppressed, I felt as if Satan pounced at the opportunity to bound me in hopelessness. I found myself in my living room surrounded by darkness with a pillow soaked with tears. I remember thinking, "God I know through faith that You are here, but I can't sense Your presence through this suffocating, life-altering moment." Before I could stop myself, I prayed to God to allow me to miscarry, if my son did in fact have Down syndrome. Just as I prayed this, I was filled with instant remorse. But God's grace showed me that His plans were bigger than my own and He was bigger than my thoughts- which were consumed with fear and were not actually true to my heart. That night, God brought me a dream that made the reality of that prayer to miscarry all too real. I found myself absolutely devastated over the loss of my son. I am so grateful for this dream because in it I found relief. The pain of losing my son was far greater than the uncertainty of his diagnosis. I awoke knowing that my baby boy was not a mistake and that my son was given to me with intention and purpose. He was a gift. It was at this moment; I knew that our story was meant to be shared for His glory.

However, this moment filled with a glimpse of hope was fleeting. The heaviness of guilt followed me heavily for months after this experience. I knew I had been forgiven by God but why did I not feel like I could forgive myself? I was haunted by thoughts such as: "I'm not a good Christian because of this. I'm a terrible mother. How could I have had this thought about my own child?" The biggest thought running through my head was, "I can't believe I reacted this way as a Christian and if I had these thoughts, how do nonbelievers survive situations such as this?"

After the birth of Emmett, I created a blog space to have the details of our experience available to other families. I prayed for the Lord to provide me a name for it. As I sat in bed one night, flipping through my bible, the words *Love That Surpasses* in Ephesians 3:19 literally jumped off the page. I knew instantly this was the name for our blog. It perfectly describes the overwhelming love of God that I have encountered during this journey. This happened in the summer of 2019, and it was right before my 29th birthday. Recently, I had seen another peer of mine from high school, post that every year on her birthday she asked God for a word for that year. I thought it was a lovely tradition and asked God for the same thing. "Lord, give me a word to hold onto and learn from during this year," I prayed. I found myself again miraculously seeing the words pop out of the page and knew that "courageous" was my word for twenty-nine.

"Have I not commanded you? Be strong and courageous. Do not be afraid; do not be discouraged, for the LORD your God will be with you wherever you go." Joshua 1:9

Shortly after we moved across the country to Silicon Valley in Northern California. Our family started new careers and made new friends. Courageous was definitely fitting for many reasons. Although it was particularly perfect due to the sudden calling which was placed on my heart to start a nonprofit in efforts to comfort others walking through a prenatal diagnosis. Strategies in business were far from what was offered in my Pediatric Nurse Practitioner didiatics. If you have never googled, "How to Start a Nonprofit," let me be the first to tell you there are laws, forms, and

A LOVE THAT SURPASSES

Courageous

so many hoops to jump through before launching. I spent all my spare time researching forms through the State of California, infrastructure of bylaws, and searching the forms on the Internal Revenue Service page. I was consumed and filled with this dream that seemed so impossible to achieve on my own. When I told my family and friends of my plans, they all agreed on how wonderful an idea it would be but then quickly reminded me of my current full-time job and not to mention how busy my two children were at home. They were absolutely right in their argument that I had zero down time. I never felt like anyone else had the same faith in this dream besides me. It was quite lonely in this exciting period and full of discouraging moments more times than I can count. I held onto my initial incorporation documents for weeks before finally bidding them farewell in the mail. I knew at that point it was going to be official and there would be no turning back. It took so much courage to finally let that letter go. There were so many thoughts that raced in my head. "Would other people think my cause was worthy?" "Would others support me?" "Would I have what it takes to keep the momentum going?" "What if I failed?"

My initial plans were to sell apparel and then create gift bags to be donated to our local genetic clinics in the Bay Area. I had walked through the whole process in about six months and decided in March of 2019 to launch and announce the nonprofit. I was so overwhelmed with the support and initial funding that was helped raised by friends, family, past, and current coworkers. I prepped donation bags for our Bags of Hope programs launch in May, when suddenly the pandemic hit. All hospitals and clinics stopped incoming donation programs and I had all of these packages for families ready to be donated with nowhere for them to go. Despite the odds, I had so much faith that the Lord would provide. I cast my social network net out wide and asked all moms on social media if they knew anyone with a prenatal diagnosis to let me know and I would ship these bags out instead of donating them. Initially, I was happy just receiving the few requests that trickled in but to my surprise things picked up very quickly. Our first year consisted of reaching more than 200 families in 36 states across the nation. We were even given the opportunity through fundraising to ship a few bags internationally. My dream was coming alive. I wouldn't have believed it if I could go back and tell myself how God paved the way for such an extraordinary outreach.

There were big steps of courage that were required to say "Yes!" to this dream God had placed on my heart. It is only natural for most people to respond out of fear when facing the unknown but what happens when we respond out of love? When you say yes to God, that's where the real magic in life happens. By choosing to respond out of love, His blessings multiply tenfold throughout our lives. My response to the unknown of my son's diagnosis was initially out of fear. Instead of letting fear imprison me unto itself, I chose the path of love. By having the courage to love others, the door was opened to help women like Shelly.

Shelly was a Christian who shared the same beliefs as me. She was in her 40's and had a long road of infertility. Her and her husband had never been able to conceive their own child and after ten years of trying decided to go the adoption route. They welcomed their son with open arms from birth. When their son was eleven years old, Shelly found to great surprise that she was pregnant. She had wanted this pregnancy so desperately and had given up this dream long ago. The term over joyous is not enough to describe their families' excitement. However, the reason that Shelly and I were connected was because of her prenatal diagnosis of Down syndrome for their son on a 13-week screening. When I found Shelly, she was at the bottom of a dark pit full of despair. "How could God lead me down such a painful road of infertility towards a heartbreaking diagnosis?" I felt an inner voice nudging me to be courageous and to share the painful parts of my story. The shameful parts. After I finished sharing the story about how I initially prayed that I would miscarry my son; she bravely admitted how this was such a relief to her. She said, "I don't even recognize myself anymore. Earlier this week I was holding my breath as the ultrasound tech was looking for my son's heartbeat because I had previously prayed that he wouldn't make it due to a miscarriage. When the tech found the heartbeat, I sighed in relief that his heart was still beating. I have been carrying such guilt afterwards though." God gave us both tender mercy that day. What was a story filled with shame became a beautiful one that was full of redemption for both Shelly and me? A few months later, Shelly reached out that she was able to share this same story with another mom who had just received a prenatal diagnosis. She was filled with joy that God had allowed her to give comfort to another in a time of despair. It is Satan's lies which tell us, "You are a terrible Christian, and you deserve to stay in this place of guilt and despair." But in God's truth, He not only forgives but through courage, He will redeem.

"Praise the Lord, my soul, and forget not all his benefits— who forgives all your sins and heals all your diseases, who redeems your life from the pit and crowns you with love and compassion," Psalms 103:2-4

Through God's abundant love and mercy, the shame of our diagnosis day was no longer there. His grace was made known through His continual presence in my journey and His love guided me towards the path of loving other people. This pivotal moment has been intricately used to glorify the kingdom of heaven. He has changed lives through our story and opened our hearts to a mission in which we seek to treat everyone with an unconditional love that mirrors the great love that Jesus has for them- where he died for all of us on the cross. Therefore, every person is worthy of love, mercy, recognition, and dignity. I literally stand in awe of God's continued blessings throughout our journey every day and the lives impacted through my simple courageous yes in faith. This freedom in truth and redemption is available to everyone who seeks it, believers and nonbelievers. Seek and you will find. Ask and it will be given to you. Dear friend, seek His courage and know that through Him all things can be redeemed. We have all sinned and fallen short of the glory of God. You have been forgiven through His love. Open your eyes to rebuke those lies, you do not have to stay imprisoned in darkness.

"Ask and it will be given to you; seek and you will find; knock and the door will be opened to you. For everyone who asks receives; the one who seeks finds; and to the one who knocks, the door will be opened." Matthew 7: 7-8

LIVING LOVED PRAYER:

"Lord, I want to become courageous through you today. I ask that in your great power, you will pour into my heart the courage of a lion and increase my faith. That through you, I ask to be free from the suffocating chains of fear, shame, and guilt. I surrender these feelings and say yes to your plans for my life today. Use my story as a powerful light of redemption for others. Guide me in your path of loving myself and others. Even if those around me are discouraging, I stand firm in my faith through you and know that you are moving mountains on my behalf for your glory. For those that ask, it will be given. For those that seek, they will find you. For those that knock, the doors will be opened. Thank you, Jesus, for renewing in me your strength today."

Dearest Friend,

Memories can either strengthen or weaken you but if we do not deal with these painful moments properly, we become captive to them. Your response was from a place of this broken world. The guilt that you carry from these early moments have taken root in the deepest parts of your heart. God has the power to remove the hurt like weeds, uproot your shame, and the crippling effects of these moments out from within our hearts. Lift your eyes to the Lord. Our all-seeing God. He longs to bring you out of this place and uplift you in His hands. Christ has forgiven you of this sin and of those thoughts.

Close your eyes and go back to that memory filled with hurt. Imagine Jesus standing there with you. What does He say to you? Meditate on this and then tell yourself, "Christ has forgiven me and now it is my turn to forgive myself." It is not your burden to carry anymore. Place this pain on His shoulders. The memory will still be there, but you are now free of the power it once held over you. Furthermore, we may have other memories from our past that also need to be addressed and healed. Take a moment to pray and ask the Holy Spirit to bring light to any other past memories from childhood to adulthood that need this same kind of healing.

Blessings,

CHAPTER SIX:
THE PERSERVERANCE OF TRUTH

"See, darkness covers the earth and thick darkness is over the peoples, but the Lord rises upon you and His glory appears over you." Isaiah 60:2

It was an ordinary sunny afternoon in Northern California, when I thought back on a conversation that I had two weeks prior. I was talking with a fellow mom friend, for the sake of privacy let's call her Mary. Mary's son also had Down syndrome and our boys are only one day apart. She will always have a special place in my heart, not only because our boys' birthdays are so close, but she was actually the first person that reached out to me on social media. Our families seemed so similar because our two oldest children are close in age as well. After going through such a long season of feeling like I couldn't relate to other couples our age who were having typical children; "meeting Mary" made me feel like ours was normal again.

One day Mary reached out over text and had mentioned something about an article she had recently read. I hadn't paid much thought at the time to this topic during Mary and I's conversation. The article was regarding a mother who had a fifty-year-old son with Down syndrome, and she spoke of her regrets. The mother in this article, stated how she wished that she would have had the opportunity to abort her son. Urging other mothers if they found out early in their pregnancy, that they should consider doing so as well. Mary expressed how terribly sad this article had made her. I gave some encouragement, but I was distracted during this moment and did not further investigate this matter. A few weeks later, I was thinking back on the conversation between Mary and I and it finally sparked my curiosity. I searched for this article and found it pretty quickly. I was prepared for the sadness that I might find by simply reading the headline but what I didn't expect were the chains of hopelessness that came thereafter.

After reading this article, I was immediately taken back to the day of our diagnosis. I found myself back in this dark pit filled with hopelessness. I began questioning if this was how I was going to feel when Emmett was older. Would I feel like my life had been stolen from me too? Would it really be so difficult and leave me with so many regrets in old age? Parenting a child with a disability is a roller coaster of emotions. Some days are so easy, and I remain confident in the value God places on our lives. Other days I am plagued by negative thoughts and feelings which seem unshakable at times. This became one of those moments for me.

As I sat on our bed, nursing Emmett, I looked into his beautiful blue eyes. I began to feel so confused by my love for him and the words that I had just read. Suddenly it hit me, who was this story line coming from? I was instantly reminded of the book that changed my life as a Christian, The Bondage Breaker by Neil Anderson. In this book, I had learned to break free from the chains that Satan binds us to by opening my eyes to see how we are unknowingly manipulated by him. His greatest tactics are to entrap through fear, anxiety, hopelessness, guilt, and shame. I realized that this definitely wasn't a story planted in God's truth but instead craftly created by Satan's hand. Immediately after this realization I prayed, "Lord, I know these feelings of hopelessness are not from you. I renounce this article for it is the work and entrapment of Satan. In the name of Jesus, these feelings be gone from me. I claim the blood of Christ over our future because in You we have hope."

Immediately, I felt the heaviness and weight of this article lift off my chest. I relinquished the fear and hopelessness back to God and it was completely gone. I peered down into my beautiful son's eyes again, and this time I was met with his love and knowing that his life was filled with purpose. I reached back out to my friend Mary immediately. Telling her how deeply disturbed I had become. She agreed and said she had felt the same way. This bright, hopeful, Christian mother ended up telling me that she had carried around the pain and worries from this article for an entire week. I was so heart wrenched to hear this from her and it left me wishing I would have read it sooner so I could have shared this freedom that I had found.

It was at this moment, I realized how many times I had felt this way throughout my parenting journey for both of my kids. The crippling fear of Hayden's communication delay and Emmett's diagnosis. The smothering guilt that followed Emmett's birth. The feelings of unfairness as it seemed that everyone else's children were always born healthy and without any

All of these thoughts that threaten our future and steal our hope; they are not from God though.

delays. The jealousy that I bottled down inside of me as friends announced their pregnancies, which were always carefree for them. All of these things are hope stealing, especially receiving any type of diagnosis for your child. These unfamiliar roads lead to unfamiliar thoughts and questions. We all walk through these new roads and experience these emotions in our own unique ways. My dear friend Mary wrote this amazing post on social media for her son on his first birthday which depicts the hopes and dreams for her son's future that she thought was lost but after much grace realized that lie. Her hopes and dreams for her unborn son were never lost and His future was always in the hands of our wonderful creator.

"Twinkle, twinkle, little star, how I wonder what you are. As I was singing my one-year-old to sleep, it hit me: my ability to dream and wonder for my boy was stolen at my prenatal diagnosis. At 13 weeks, when parents are eagerly awaiting the gender reveal, we were handed statistics and apologies. When we left the doctors, we were met with assumptions. "He will be like this... He will not do that. He will live there." The mystery taken; the unknown revealed. Conversations about future college and career came to a halt. But I do wonder, and I do dream, ever since I held you in my arms. You have reclaimed my stolen dreams and have returned them to me: "Here they are, Mama; these belong to you." I see it in your eyes every time you disprove misconceptions: you urge me to wait and see. Your future is just as full of mystery and possibility as any typical child. Your path is not determined, and I will fight with you and for your dreams."

All of these thoughts that threaten our future and steal our hope; they are not from God though. They are lies fed to us by Satan who is trying to keep us distant from truth, hope, and being brave. Once we unveil our eyes to this scheme, we are able to realize that through Jesus we have hope and most importantly we have freedom.

Uphold that fear, pain, hopelessness, and submit them to the cross in Jesus' name. Because He has already conquered all of those strongholds. The day that He died on the cross, was the day that death and the strongholds which are the works of Satan, were overcome. Satan is all but an illusion of a great roaring lion who cowards and submits to the name of Jesus. Hebrews 2:14-15 speaks of how Christ came to share in our humanity so that by death, He would obtain the power over the one who holds the keys to death, which is Satan. In Jesus, your freedom has been given to you as an inheritance, but Satan will do anything in his power to make you think otherwise. This truth is real friends and it's powerful. Most importantly, this truth will set you free.

"He reveals the deep things of darkness and brings utter darkness into the light." Job 12:22

"Since the children have flesh and blood, he too shared in their humanity so that by his death he might break the power of him who holds the power of death—that is, the devil— and free those who all their lives were held in slavery by their fear of death." Hebrews 2:14-15

LIVING LOVED PRAYER:

"Jesus, thank you for conquering death for me. It is through Your resurrection that we are freed. Please open my eyes to see what situation and thoughts Satan is holding me captive over. Give me your peace today from these things which brew turmoil in my heart. I rebuke _____ (insert your own feelings and situation here) in your name Jesus. I recognize that these feelings are not from you. I am believing in Your power; I am freed of this. I claim the blood of Jesus Christ over my future because in You we have hope."

CHAPTER SEVEN:
TRADING JEALOUSY FOR JOY

"Although you have been forsaken and hated, with no one traveling through, I will make you the everlasting pride and the joy of all generations." Isaiah 60:15

This alternative parenting journey that I have found myself walking is continuously surprising me with deep seeded hurts. Hurts like jealousy that seems to be secretly hiding in my heart. Now hear me out, I love my children with every fiber of my being. I will fight for them to be loved and respected for who they are until the end. However, it's hard to fully explain the emotion that hits you out of nowhere when faced with certain triggers.

A big trigger for me is hearing other women announcing their pregnancy. Usually, their pregnancy is uneventful, and their screenings are normal. They go on to grow beautiful big bellies, daydream about painting nurseries, and picking out the right names. It feels like they all go onto having the typical experiences of motherhood without any regards to therapies, specialist appointments, or having conversations about milestone delays. When I am in a triggering situation it hits me so hard. If I am being completely honest, I feel robbed of this normal experience. I know others feel it too from conversations with my husband to other parents who are in different but similar situations. All of us vocalize at some point how we feel robbed. If you are feeling these thoughts too, I want you to know that you are not alone. I want to be transparent that I have not perfected this topic in my life but would like to shed some truth that has encouraged me along the way.

The enemy loves to use other people's words to hold power over us. This strategy is Satan's favorite because in doing so, this keeps us from moving forward and embracing God's calling in our lives. After being in a triggering situation on a particular day, my dear friend Megan encouraged me to not doubt myself by saying how amazing, capable, strong, courageous, brave, beautiful, purposeful, skilled, and determined I am. While I appreciated the life-giving words it wasn't these things that I doubted. It was the heaviness of jealousy that sat down on my chest like an elephant, and it blinded me from my joy. Jealousy makes us believe that we missed out on something better than what we have and covering our eyes in darkness from the truth. When I spiral down this road, I typically encourage myself to take a step back from these thoughts and think about if my life had turned out the way I'd envisioned it. In doing this, I realize how I wouldn't be having this conversation with Megan. We had met because of my calling to start Love that Surpasses Ministries which was inspired by my son. I would not have half as many meaningful friendships. In fact, the friendships I have obtained through the Down syndrome community made a huge difference in my life when we moved across the country. I definitely think that our move to California would have been harder and more isolating without these friendships.

However, sometimes these thoughts aren't enough though to pick up that elephant of jealousy and lift it off my chest. On one particular day I was faced by a triggering situation of a coworker announcing her pregnancy. This morning before my shift I had my morning quiet time with God and reflected back on the previous night. I had recently been seeing different time sequences on the clock. These continuous sightings in numbers sparked my attention about a month previously and in particular the 11:11 sequence. I had a friend say that when she would see this number on the clock, she associated it with Hebrews 11:11 in the bible which states; "And by faith even Sarah, who was past childbearing age, was enabled to bear children because she considered him faithful who had made the promise." Essentially, every time I see this number, I too think of this verse, which is filled with God's miracles and promises.

This wasn't the number sequence that I saw that night though. The number on the clock that stood out to me that night was 5:55 and it was actually one that I had never seen before. In fact, I remember being so off guard by this one that I made a mental note of it to search the bible later for an answer. My search landed in Isaiah 55:5, which speaks of the Lord endowing us with splendor. In more than one circumstance, the Lord has been calling my attention to Isaiah chapter 54 and so that morning I felt compelled to read both chapters. I became captivated by Isaiah 54, which

Take comfort that in Him, we have all been chosen and predestined according to the purpose of His will.

encourages the barren women to burst into song and shout for joy because more are the children from her as a desolate woman than those who have a husband.

"Sing, barren woman, you who never bore a child; burst into song, shout for joy, you who were never in labor; because more are the children of the desolate woman than of her who has a husband," says the Lord. "Enlarge the place of your tent, stretch your tent curtains wide, do not hold back; lengthen your cords, strengthen your stakes. For you will spread out to the right and to the left; your descendants will dispossess nations and settle in their desolate cities." Isaiah 54: 1-3

When I received Emmett's prenatal diagnosis, one of the first thoughts I had was that he would never produce offspring. I was so incredibly sad that I would never have any grandchildren from him. Looking back on those moments, I always thought this was such a weird thing for an expecting mother to be thinking of her grandchildren. Most boys with Down syndrome are born sterile and I heavily grieved this. My grief was rooted from the desire in my heart to have a big family. Growing up, it was just my younger brother and me. I dreamed of having at least three children and a handful of grandkids. I wanted a big house to celebrate the holidays with everyone. A house that was filled with my children and all of theirs running around. The thoughts of being stripped of this dream were crushing. While barrenness represents misfortune and unfruitfulness, I felt as if the Lord was speaking this verse to say, "Sarah, sing and shout for joy, even though I have made Emmett barren; you will be blessed and stretch your house in ways that are not possible for others."

I had meditated on this scripture immediately before being placed in a situation where jealousy filled my spirit. I knew that the Lord had prepared my heart for that moment through these words of scripture. Instead of having to battle jealousy in my heart that day I surrendered all of these feelings to Him. The Lord replaced my hurts with His truth, peace, and promises of blessings. Take comfort that in Him, we have all been chosen and predestined according to the purpose of His will. (Ephesians 1:11) I encourage you to ask Him to reveal these blessings in your life and surrender your hurt feelings for His peace. We can hold onto His promises of abundance that He speaks of in Isaiah 55, *"You will go out in joy and be led forth in peace; the mountains and the hills will burst into song before you, and all the trees of the field will clap their hands. Instead of the thornbush will grow juniper, and instead of the briers the myrtle will grow. This will be for the Lord's renown, for an everlasting sign, that will endure forever."*

LIVING LOVED PRAYER:

"Lord, I surrender these thoughts and feelings of jealousy in my heart to you. Replace in me these feelings of jealousy, anger, and sadness with your peace. Thank you for giving me a joyful heart instead and filling it with your love. Heal these wounds and use them for your glory. Open my eyes to see how you have provided and blessed me with an abundance of more in my life. In Jesus' name, I renounce the jealousy in my heart to flee from me and I claim joy over the path you have led me to. So be it. Amen."

CHAPTER EIGHT:
GOD ON DISPLAY

Jesus said, "but this happened so that the works of God might be displayed in him."
John 9:3

After I received my non-invasive prenatal test results (NIPT), we were referred to an ultrasound appointment for further measurements. I remember so clearly my husband was sitting to my left. Our stomachs were both in knots as we sat in the dimmed light of the waiting room. I watched as another couple who was expecting came out and the mother was sobbing. Instinctively, I wanted to comfort her. I wondered if she had just received a Down syndrome diagnosis as well or perhaps something worse such as news that her baby didn't make it. After the ultrasound was complete, we were led into this room which had a very large conference table in the shape of an oval. It was where my husband and I would be meeting with the genetic counselor. I remember thinking that the table was way too large for the three of us. My husband and I held our breaths for the news that was about to come as we sat across from her. She began to explain that there were soft markers present and while these findings were not 100% diagnostic, the likelihood that our son was to have Down syndrome was 99% based on all the screenings. She began the sentence that we should talk about our options. I remember being horrified by where this conversation was going and saying that there were no options for us. We were going to be welcoming our son regardless of his chromosomes. Her solemn tone changed, and I could see her sigh in relief that she didn't have to walk down that road either. She proceeded to provide us information that she could connect us with other families in the area who had children with Down syndrome to talk with. However, if I am being honest, I wasn't ready to face that this was going to be our reality yet and declined her kind offer.

As a healthcare provider, I was aware that Trisomy 21 was typically due to an extra chromosome from the mother's egg. While there is a small chance that it could be from the father's sperm, that's typically not the case.

There is no explanation as to why this happens, and no one is at fault or to blame. Even knowing this answer, I still felt the need to look our genetic counselor in the eyes and ask her, "Did I do something in pregnancy to cause this?" My husband turned to look at me with a scrunched look on his face because he knew that I knew this answer. Our genetic counselor reassured me that trisomy 21 is a random event. I was not at fault for this occurrence. This answer left me so dissatisfied. I wanted to have an answer as to why it occurred. I needed a reason and a cause for this event. I couldn't shake these thoughts and wanted someone to desperately tell me why this had happened to me. Why me?

We declined doing further diagnostic testing that would give us firm results of his extra chromosome, which left us with only high screening results. We wouldn't know for a fact that our son would be born with Down syndrome until the day of his birth. This unknown gave me days that I could live in disbelief that this was happening to us, and other days certain songs would trigger me. Sending me into a downward spiral of sobbing while driving. Sometimes I would close my eyes at night to envision what our expanding family would look like in a professional photograph. Every time, I always saw the four of us and on top of my husband's shoulders he would be holding our son who had Down syndrome. I always found so much peace when envisioning this family picture because we were all very happy. There were no feelings of sadness associated in this vision. In fact, when I tried to envision our son without Down syndrome, I would feel sadness. Even then, this question always remained, "Why was this happening to me?"

It would take me almost three years later, after sitting across the table from the genetic counselor, to have that question answered. I was driving into work and had decided to turn on my hometown church podcast. It was springtime and we were in the season of Lent. This series was about the signs and miracles Jesus performed during His ministry on earth leading up to the cross. The sixth miracle Jesus performed was the healing of a blind man. It says in John, chapter 9, Jesus saw a man who had been blind since his birth but what caught my attention about this story is the disciples' reaction to this

It is so the deeds of God may be on display.

man. They immediately asked Jesus, "Who has sinned to cause this? This man or his family?" Even the ones who were closest and walked alongside Jesus during His time on earth were thinking the same exact thoughts in my head as I learned about my son which was "Why did this happen and who's fault is it?" They were trying to explain away this brokenness because surely there must be a logical reason that this man has had to suffer and carry around this pain from birth. We still find ourselves so often thinking this way. We carry around the guilt and shame from something that's not our fault at all. This thought process is not specific to the Down syndrome community either. I can only imagine that parents receiving a diagnosis of autism, PANS, or cancer (just to name a few) would feel this way as well.

Jesus provides not only physical healing for this man but in the greater picture of this story, has provided us with an incredible spiritual healing by giving us the answer to our question in this same passage. He says why the man was born blind by telling His disciples that neither this man nor his family sinned. Jesus is saying it's not this man's fault and his blindness cannot be explained. His blindness cannot be traced to anyone's sin. Since the fall of mankind in Genesis, when sin entered into the world, we are now living in a broken world. A world now that consists of broken things and broken people. Jesus didn't come to necessarily prevent the brokenness from happening, but He did come to restore it and give us the answer. He tells his disciples that the reason this man is blind is so the deeds of God may be put on display. This powerful truth that this story has to offer is uncovering the lie in your heart that is telling you a painful event must be your fault. However, in Jesus' truth, you stand firm through His word that says your pain, brokenness, struggle, and blindness is not due to any fault of our own. It is so the deeds of God may be on display. In this same token, God doesn't cause our suffering. It is a product of this broken world that we live in but what He can do is use our suffering to display His glory. You only need to have the spiritual lens to see this mighty work.

Furthermore, this miracle about Jesus healing the blind man was never about his physical blindness and was much bigger than this man. It was about the spiritual blindness of mankind. We would have never walked the path of these situations that caused us pain, but we can find comfort in that place through a fresh new heavenly perspective that will bring us peace, comfort, and freedom. Once our eyes are free from the spiritual blinders, we realize for the first time, how broken we all are but most importantly, how deep and wide and long and high is the love and grace of Jesus.

LIVING LOVED PRAYER:

"Lord, I bring my hurting heart to you today. For too long, I have carried the burden of blame. I give you my pain and brokenness today. I praise you for taking these chains from me. Today, I choose to no longer live in these feelings by relinquishing them in your name Jesus. Fill me with your peace and show me the light of your glory in my life. Amen."

CHAPTER NINE:
A LOVE THAT SURPASSES

"You shall know the truth and the truth shall set you free."
John 8:32

I have always been extremely sensitive to atmosphere changes and the most drastic change that I have ever experienced was the day of Emmett's diagnosis. After the phone call, I found myself in my living room amongst a thick fog of darkness. I clearly remember thinking, "Lord, I know you are here but why can't I feel you? Where are you?"

Being in Christ, I stood in my faith that God is always with us even in the darkest of moments but even as Christians we are not exempted from Satan's battle of our minds. It is only through Christ's truth, that we can resist these lies and maintain our freedom. Though we might be surrounded by darkness; His love for us is all encompassing and omnipresent. I felt the promise of His love like a fire during these devastating moments. People who have disabilities are often viewed as less, broken, defective thorough worldly standards. However, this is not God's truth. Paul's prayer for the Ephesians speaks of Christs' love for us which is wide and long and high and deep. This love has no restrictions for certain individuals. Christs' love is for everyone. No exceptions.

"I pray that out of his glorious riches he may strengthen you with power through his Spirit in your inner being, so that Christ may dwell in your hearts through faith. And I pray that you, being rooted and established in love, may have power, together with all the Lord's holy people, to grasp how wide and long and high and deep is the love of Christ, and to know this love that surpasses knowledge—that you may be filled to the measure of all the fullness of God. Now to him who is able to do immeasurably more than all we ask or imagine, according to his power that is at work within us." Ephesians 3: 16-20

Christs' love is for everyone.

I knew that this demonstration of Christs' love was the foundation that I wanted Love That Surpasses Ministries to be built on. Through His love, we obtain in abundance more than we could ever ask or imagine. We obtain truth and freedom from darkness through His love.

What if I told you that you don't have to live in the lies of guilt, anger, fear, jealousy, and bitterness anymore? Your mind is a battlefield, but once we accept Jesus as our savior; freedom is your inheritance. If you are not a Christian reading this book, you might be wondering about the first steps that need to be taken to obtain this love and freedom. It is as simple as accepting Christ as the Son of God and that He died on the cross and rose again. It's knowing that Jesus' love for you surpasses your own understanding. Because of this love, He has died on the cross to be able to spend eternity with you. He has bridged the gap between us and sin, forever. Nothing can separate you, me, us from His love. Nothing.

"Because, if you confess with your mouth that Jesus is Lord and believe in your heart that God raised him from the dead, you will be saved." Romans 10:9

"But God demonstrates his own love for us in this: While we were still sinners, Christ died for us." Romans 5:8

Our battle with darkness has been won when Jesus died on the cross, but Satan will do anything to make us believe it hasn't been. Just because you have taken this first step does not mean that the battle is over. Even Christians find themselves surrounded in a battle against these lies. I know I did for a very long time which is why writing this book has been placed on my heart so heavily. The next step after committing yourself to Christ, is recognizing WHO your thoughts are coming from and standing firm in your rightful inheritance through Him. Our key is this, because of Christ' death and resurrection every believer is made alive IN HIM. By accepting Jesus into our lives, He resides IN US through the holy spirit. We do not need any kind of outside agent to assert authority for us because we now reside in Christ. I wish I would have learned this crucial power that is given to us by the holy spirit through our baptism a long time ago. It's such a crucial weapon in our walk with Christ and in our daily lives. In 1 John chapter four, it talks about testing the spirits because not every spirit is from God. This chapter gives us hope in victory over false thoughts and spirits by saying, *"Little children, you are from God and have overcome them, for he who is in you is greater than he who is in the world." 1 John 4:4*

By taking a step back from negative thoughts and holding each one captive; not only are our eyes opened to decipher the devils' deceit, but we can now fight back against it. A prime example in my life, when Emmett was six months old, we attended church one Sunday. I watched my daughter play after Sunday school with all the other children on the playground, when out of nowhere I started frantically looking at the other children. I was scanning the playground full of children looking to see if any of them had Down syndrome in an effort to not feel alone. The thoughts that immediately filled my head were deceitful such as: "All their children are perfect." "You don't belong here." "None of these parents can relate to you." "You have been cast aside." I remember immediately texting another mom friend whose child has Down syndrome as well and asked if she ever felt this way. We agreed that we both did, and it seemed to be just a part of processing the diagnosis. I wish that I could go back to that moment. Because if I could go back and tell myself one thing it would be "Sarah, take those thoughts captive.

Who is telling you these things?" The ability to realize who is feeding you these lies is life changing. Suddenly I realized just how easily Satan deceives and oppresses the disability community. Not only this community but my eyes were opened to how easily a diagnosis is used to isolate individuals and bury families in lies. Satan loves to isolate, corner, and make us think there is no hope and that we have been cast aside. My heart hurts for those that are blinded by these untruths and reside in internal turmoil. My hope is that your eyes would be opened and able to see how heavily we as Christians can be deceived. Even more importantly, how easy it is to overcome it and stand firm in your rightful inheritance. Are you thinking that you are not a good enough Christian? That's a lie. Are you thinking that this will never work for you? Whoa, that's a lie. Are you thinking (insert negative thought here)? Again, lies. It's time to tell Satan and all his clever schemes to take a seat. You reside in Christ and His power in you. That same power that's defeated death. It's time to take back your life by living in Christ's love and freedom. Nothing can separate us now from His love, remember?

"For I am convinced that neither death nor life, neither angels nor demons, neither the present nor the future, nor any powers, neither height nor depth, nor anything else in all creation, will be able to separate us from the love of God that is in Christ Jesus our Lord." Romans 8:38-39

LIVING LOVED PRAYER:

"Thank you, Lord, for the promise of Your unconditional love for me. Help me to rest in your truth today that neither the present nor future, nor any powers, height nor depth, nor anything else in all creation, can separate me from your love. I surrender my life to you and rest in your love today."

A LOVE THAT SURPASSES

Dearest Friend,

    All too often, we find ourselves peering into social situations and hear an accusatory voice telling us, "They don't want to be my friend." I am especially guilty of this as a female. It might seem easy to see this lie while reading these words. However, at the moment, this accusatory voice is often very loud and isolating. "You'll never fit in." "They won't understand you." "You aren't welcome here." "They don't want to hire you." "You aren't good enough." Does this voice sound familiar? If we listen to this voice for long enough it will start sounding like our own but take a step back to ask yourself where these lies are coming from. The enemy's main goal is to isolate us. Satan will do almost anything to put you into a corner and strip you of your birthright in Christ which is love and worth. He accomplishes this ever so sneakily. The voice in your head which sounds like your own. First starting softly but growing ever so loudly.

    Oftentimes, this feeling of being cast aside is more intense as a parent of a child with a disability. However, think back to before having your child and maybe not knowing anyone with a disability. It's not that you didn't want to be friends with these families. No, you wouldn't feel this way at all. At that time, you were just naive and unaware of HOW to approach this relationship. So as parents of children with a disability, let us approach others whose eyes have not been opened to our world and invite them in with grace. Let's change the script of isolation, by extending grace to others whose eyes and ears have not yet been exposed to the disability community. By taking the stance and standing in Christs' truth; we stand strong against the enemy who feeds us lies in hopes of isolating us. Freedom from chains of isolation is your inheritance!

Blessings,

CHAPTER TEN:
LIVING LOVED

"I sought the Lord, and he answered me; he delivered me from all my fears. Those who look to him are radiant; their faces are never covered with shame." Psalms 34:4-5

The hardest part about parenting a child with a disability is not the child themselves or their diagnosis. In fact, loving them is so natural and easy. It's navigating people's reactions and ignorant comments, which tend to be pretty common, and it becomes painfully repetitive. Most of the time people act or say things oblivious to their dependence on superficial societal norms, while other times, people intentionally reject your child and their disabilities. All because it doesn't fit in their own mold. It's a heart wrenching internal battle for us as parents because when they dismiss your child; they renounce you as well. Deep in our hearts a big fear that is associated with a disability diagnosis is one that's rooted in utter loneliness and rejection. Are you able to step outside of moments like these and realize the lie associated with this? Are you able to recognize the codependency of a broken view and look to Jesus and His definition of all of us? As I grew more in dismantling these lies, I found it to be very beneficial to ask myself these questions, not only in response to situations regarding the rejection of my son but my daughter as well.

In fact, there was a situation with my daughter that left me feeling so discouraged I was so full of anger after an individualized education plan meeting (IEP) for Hayden to receive speech therapy services that I had a hard time shaking it. As I sat across from the team, it felt like they were just nonchalantly walking through the check boxes and approaching her behavior as a standard, rather than as an individual. It was certainly a heart wrenching moment, because as her mother, I knew what she was truly capable of and their overview did not line up with what I believed to be true. I felt as if they saw her minor differences as enough justification to lump her into a much larger category that did speak to her unique needs. It all felt so dismissive. It seemed like my sweet Hayden was just a number to them, being cast aside as they moved on to the next child on their schedule. Devalued is the perfect word that I felt at this moment. I remember after the meeting praying to God, asking Him to provide forgiveness in my heart because they were not aware of their desensitization and that their approach was hurtful.

Doesn't this story sound familiar? Let us not forget this is exactly what happened to Jesus. He was rejected by his own people. Oh, how heartbroken God was by this rejection of His son. But when Jesus died on the cross, He cried out to God, "Father, forgive them. They do not understand what they are doing." (Luke 23:24) How true is this statement still today, especially in the world of disabilities? Due to ignorance, people are unaware of what they are doing is harmful and how it is fueled by sin. I'm not sure that this vicious cycle will ever end and seems to be a product of our broken world. It was around when Jesus was here, and it is still happening daily. Parenting any child can be an ongoing battle with Satan because he loves to use rejection from other people to isolate and leave us bitter and alone. Even Jesus acknowledges how Satan uses others and their words against us. When Jesus was telling His disciples that He would die on the cross for God's glory, Peter begs him to change his mind. *Jesus turned and said to Peter, "Get behind me, Satan! You are a stumbling block to me; you do not have in mind the concerns of God, but merely human concerns." Matthew 16:23*

So how do we arm ourselves in truth to face this broken system? How do we continue to walk down this path we have been called to with strength? How do we avoid the burning arrows that are aimed towards our heart with a mission to fill us with bitterness? Our answer lies in digging deeper into our relationship with Jesus. By asking Him to open our eyes to His truths, we can be joyful and stand firm in Him. Now after finding the truth, my heart is thankful as I pray, "I rejoice and praise you. For I am joyful amidst the rejection which I face because in You my eyes are opened versus those who are still blind and fumbling in the dark." There is thanksgiving to be found, for once we were blind but now, we are seeing! You are a light which has been turned on and once we find ourselves shining, we realize just how dark it was in that place--the place that many others are still dwelling. *"I will lead the blind by ways they have not known, along unfamiliar paths I will guide them; I will turn the darkness into light before them and make the rough places smooth. These are the things I will do; I will not forsake them." Isaiah 42:16*

Lastly, live loved because you are — deeply!

In this last chapter, I would like to share my own prayer strategy to help you maintain your rightful inheritance of freedom in Christ. Make sure that you didn't miss out on the first steps of this process in Chapter nine, which is to accept Jesus' love and to stand firm in it. Lastly, live loved because you are— deeply!

Daily Steps to Living Loved in Christs' Love That Surpasses
1. **Putting on your armor!**

We have been given the authority to come against the enemy who will try to exert a negative influence over our lives. At times we may have opened doors to those influences and it's time to close these. The enemy is very clever at staying hidden behind the lies that it projects towards you. Feeling fearful, hopeless, angry, or anxious? These are not the voices of God and is why Paul says in 2 Corinthians 2:5 to "take every thought captive." Let's reclaim our freedom in Christ back and live in His truth!

"Be strong in the Lord and in His mighty power. Put on the full armor of God so that you can take your stand against the devil's schemes." Ephesians 6:12

"Heavenly Father, I declare your protection and the blood of Jesus over myself and my family. I put on God's armor including the buckle of truth around my waist, integrity for a breastplate, the shield of faith, and the helmet of truth. I stand firm in faith and the Lord's armor to resist Satan's tactics. Show me where Satan has a hold on my life and forgive me for intentionally or unintentionally partnering with the enemy. I choose to reclaim any territory that I have handed over to Satan by placing it in the Lord's hands. I claim freedom in Christ over my mind and thoughts and rebuke Satan and all of his empty words. In the name of Jesus, I bind any spirit of <u>(anger, jealousy, guilt, hopelessness, fear, unforgiveness, and shame)</u> away from me now. Thank you, Lord, for setting me free and replacing in my heart your love and peace. Amen."

2. **Be still and know through prayers of surrender.**

When we surrender our hearts to Christ, we let Him come into the deepest places of our lives and mold those broken pieces back together. He will fill our lives with a great and surpassing peace. Let us pray for humility and surrender our everything to Him. Psalms 46:10 says, "Be still and know that I am God."

"Humble yourselves before the Lord, and he will lift you up." James 4:10.

"Lord, I surrender to you today. Come into my life in a deeper way and light up all of the corners of my heart. I hold nothing back and surrender my (marriage, occupation, children, successes, failures, health, etc.). I surrender my pride today and ask to be filled with your humility. I surrender my entire life, past, present and future to you Lord. I am yours. Thank you for coming into my life in a deeper way-making a lasting change in me. Amen."

3. **No longer Guilty: Liberation through repentance.**

Sin can hold us back from having a deeper relationship with God. When we repent, we open ourselves up to freedom from guilt making us more aware of His unconditional love for us. When I entered the road of "different parenting," my initial thoughts were those of a sinner. Through my repentance, I laid down my unworthiness to pick up Christs' surpassing forgiveness and He has opened my eyes to see how He loves us. Every one of us. No exceptions.

"If we claim to be without sin, we deceive ourselves and the truth is not in us. If we confess our sins, he is faithful and just and will forgive us our sins and purify us from all unrighteousness." 1 John 1:8-9

"I come before you Lord with a repentant heart. I have sinned in my thoughts and actions. I repent for the lack of faith, doubt, and especially _____ (insert your personal struggle(s). Please bring to my mind any sin that I have done which is blocking the flow of your love towards me. I repent of this today. I no longer hide from you today and I accept your forgiveness. Open my eyes to see your all-surpassing love for me and pour out your blessings into my life by showering me in your truths

today. Thank you for liberating and healing me today. Amen."

4. **The Healing of Forgiveness.**

The forgiveness of others is a huge step in the liberation process. You cannot move into God's love and freedom with bitterness in your heart towards others. When you were only worthy of death, Jesus forgave you of everything so that not only may you live in freedom during this life but also have eternal life. However, in exchange, He wants you to extend this love to others who don't deserve it too. This can be a very hard step but make a list of everyone who has hurt you. Even the deepest hurts that you cannot forgive by your own strength is not too big for Jesus. I encourage you to ask for His strength in the forgiving process to intercede on your behalf.

"Be kind to one another, tenderhearted, forgiving one another, as God in Christ forgave you." Ephesians 4:32

"Father, I am choosing to forgive _____(insert person or past self) of their wrong doings against me, just as you have graciously chosen to forgive me. I extend this same grace through you today to that person. Please bring to mind others who have hurt me in the past so that I may forgive them today as well. Jesus, there are those who have hurt me too deeply to forgive through my own strength. I ask that You intercede on my behalf and through Your strength Jesus _____ may be forgiven in my heart for all their wrong doings towards me. I understand that a bitter heart blocks the flow of your love to me. Open the floodgates of your love today through the forgiveness in my heart of others. In Jesus name, Amen."

5. **Praising His Goodness with a Thankful Heart.**

When we praise and thank Him, we are always drawn deeper in our faith. Praising and thanking God, builds confidence and belief in His movement and power. Let us praise Him for the continual splendor He lavishes on us.

"The Lord is my strength and my shield; My heart trusts in Him, and I am helped; Therefore, my heart exults, and with my song I shall thank Him." Psalms 28:7

"Thank you, Lord, for drawing me closer to you today. Thank you for giving me the power to overcome old habits and negative thoughts in you today. Thank you for encouraging me to walk in the light of joy. Thank you for the grace to lean on your understanding and not my own. Thank you for pouring out your blessings on my life. Thank you for the wonderful gift of my life. Thank you for healing my heart and soul from the inside out. Let your light shine through me today. I praise you Jesus, the wonderful redeemer. I praise you Jesus for healing me by Your liberation today. Amen."

Dearest Friend,

Many of you know the story of Jesus' request of God for forgiveness towards the people who sentenced Him to death. In Luke 23:24, Jesus said those famous words, "Father, forgive them, for they do not know what they are doing." You might find yourself thinking, "Well He was able to forgive the people who had hurt him so badly because He is God's son. I have not been given this strength to forgive my accusers." But have you heard the story of Stephen? In Acts 7:54-60, Stephen, a man of God, cried out to the Lord while he was being stoned to death for His Father to forgive them. Stephen, who is an ordinary man just like you and I, while dying one of the most painful deaths finds the strength in his heart to cry out to God for the forgiveness of his accusers. I want you to think of the person who has hurt you the most. The person that your heart is wounded so deeply by that there is no possible way you could ever forgive them. Ordinary Stephen wasn't able to do this on his own either. What made ordinary Stephen so extraordinary is that he was empowered by the Holy Spirit!

Some of us have received the Holy Spirit in Baptism but we have not utilized it yet. Through the empowerment and strength of the Holy Spirit we are able to forgive anyone. Through our activation of the Holy Spirit: He establishes our identity, He shows us our value in the kingdom of God, He reveals our path and purpose, He leads us into truth, He heals us, and the wounds that have been inflicted upon us through sin. I declare the greatness of God to be poured out over you today. Ask the Holy Spirit to pour out on you so that you may know His love and rest in the Great Comforters arms daily. The one who hears the heart's cries earnestly seeks to heal you daily and the biggest healing that we could ever receive is the activation of the Holy Spirit within us. My biggest advice to you is to pray without ceasing for this outpouring event where the fire of Christ ignites in your heart. This movement of God will transform your whole life.

Blessings,

Sarah

ABOUT THE AUTHOR

Sarah is a Nashville, Tennessee native who currently resides in the San Francisco Bay area with her family. She is the mother of two joyful children, Hayden and Emmett. Sarah loves hiking, good brunch spots, and deep conversations. Her heart longs to help others find their way out of darkness and into the light of Christ. She is a certified Pediatric Nurse Practitioner, Founder, and Chief Executive Officer of Love that Surpasses Ministries. The most important job to her though is the one where she is called "mommy."

For more information about Love that Surpasses Ministries and resources for families, please visit our website or check us out on social media:

www.lovethatsurpasses.org
@lovethatsurpassesministries

Made in the USA
Middletown, DE
15 August 2022